About Danielle MacKinnon

'm a Soul Level Animal Communicator®, Intuitive and Soul
Level Intuitive Coach®. I've been connecting psychically
with animals here and on the Other Side for more than two
decades. In my Danielle MacKinnon School, established in
2004, I've taught students from more than sixty countries
how to use my trademarked method, called Soul Level
Animal Communication® to communicate with their pets,
both alive and deceased.

Now, I want to share my many years of experience to
help you feel better about your pet on the Other Side—and
perhaps even connect with them.

THE
Incredible Animal
AFTERLIFE

THE
Incredible Animal
AFTERLIFE

What **Your Pet** Wants
You to Know

by

DANIELLE MACKINNON

animal intuitive

For information about this title or to order other books and/or electronic media, contact the publisher:

MacKinnon Media, Inc.
Daniellemackinnon.com
info@daniellemackinnon.com

ISBNs:
979-8-218-08404-2 (softcover)
979-8-218-05181-5 (eBook)

Printed in the United States of America

Art Direction/Cover Concept + Design: Carolyn Gerin
Cover Illustrator: Kim Lincon

Dedicated to Kevin

How to use this book

I have written this book to address the most common questions I receive about animals and the Other Side. You can use this book in one of three ways:

1. Read it cover to cover. This will give you the best overall understanding of the animal afterlife and how things work for your beloved pet. *I recommend this option!*

2. Use the chapter titles to dive into a specific area of the animal afterlife.

3. In the Table of Contents, I've made it easy to scan through to see each question I've covered. Use the Table of Contents to find the exact answer you're looking for.

Contents

CHAPTER 1

THE BIG PICTURE

Why this loss hurts so much

I feel like I have been taken advantage of.
It's only a dog.

—Danielle's former employer

"I feel like I have been taken advantage of. It's only a dog." I heard this when I returned to my corporate job at a Fortune 500 company after three days home grieving the loss of my dog, Mabel. Usually, my boss wasn't uncaring; however, she seemed genuinely perplexed and perturbed by my overwhelm and grief surrounding the passing of my dog. Naive comments like this can make losing a beloved animal family member more challenging than losing a human family member. You end up feeling like no one understands.

I'm sure you've heard comments like:

- You're STILL upset about your cat?

- It's not like it's your child.

- He couldn't even talk!

- Get over it. It's just an animal.

For me (and I'm sure you if you're reading this), I trust the animals in my life more than most of my friends and family. Unfortunately, not everyone feels this way, which makes it very hard for them to understand the great loss people like us feel when our beloved animals die.

After twenty-plus years of working intuitively with people and their pets here and on the Other Side, I've seen that gaining a spiritual understanding of the animal death and dying process can assist with a lot of the loneliness, pain, and hurt. This understanding won't magically heal all grief. Still, it will soften the edges and provide a road map for being in connection with your beloved pet again.

The Role of Animals and Mass Consciousness

To understand the animal death and dying process, we must first appreciate the role of living animals and mass consciousness.

Animals experience life at two different levels.

The first level is the one we're all familiar with: the physical. Here, an animal can feel jealousy, anger, pain, suffering, and happiness. As we expect, animals will simply do everything in their power to survive. We see this when we witness a cat running away from a dog or a horse seeking food.

The second level focuses on my work with animals—the Soul Level®. Here, every animal has access to an expansive awareness beyond their physical survival. They know:

- Why they are incarnated

- Why you are incarnated

- What you need to do to be the happiest, healthiest person you can be

- What they need to do to help you achieve that

- What human consciousness needs to evolve, and much more.

It's from the Soul Level® perspective that animals mastermind their lives here with us on Earth to assist us.

At first, it may seem hard to believe that animals possess the spiritual chops to plan their physical lives and deaths. After all, two chipmunks playing chase through the woods don't exactly look all that spiritually evolved! But, that deep, Soul Level wisdom really is there. I know because I've tapped into it tens of thousands of times in my animal communication readings, and I've been teaching my students to do the same for years.

At the Soul Level®, animals have mastered unconditional love. This is why they are so forgiving and why, left to their own devices, they eventually find balance within themselves and their environment. In nature, squirrels don't question their worth as good squirrels, fish don't feel bad about themselves for being slow swimmers, and birds don't reprimand themselves for not catching their prey. While at the physical level, animals want to survive, at the Soul Level®, they want to take their mastery of unconditional love and share it with us (humans) so we, too, can grow and evolve.

By intuitively tapping into our Soul Level® to find out what we most need, animals assist our daily growth. Whereas we humans can spend decades trying to figure out what will make us finally feel happy or fulfilled, animals innately know this about us. They bark at our postal carrier to remind us to use our voice, suffer anxiety to hold a mirror to our panic, and they inspire in us great love and trust as we have never felt before. However they choose to do it, animals use their bodies, minds, behaviors, and alignment with unconditional love to illuminate what they know needs illuminating within us.

Here's an example of how my dog Bella used her love for me to help me grow and evolve when she was alive:

Bella was my misbehaving, jumping up and down chocolate lab who often drove my husband and me nuts. This was
a long time ago when I was a budding animal communicator
and my belief then was that, if I was any good at my job,
I should be able to control her behavior psychically. Mind
control did not work, though; the more she jumped on people,
the worse I felt about myself as an animal communicator.

While, at the physical level, Bella was just an exuberant
lab who loved all people, at the Soul Level, she was actively
trying to stimulate and highlight my self-worth challenges
around my chosen profession. And she continued to do this
as long as I did not value my skills at my work. Interestingly,
the more I accepted that there was no way I was ever going
to be able to psychically control Bella (because psychic mind
control is not a thing), and accepted and enjoyed her for
whom she was, without it being a reflection on my goodness,
the less she jumped up on people. By the time Bella died, I
believed in myself as an animal communicator and loved
Bella for who she was. And instead of jumping up on visitors,
she would bring them a teddy bear or mitten in greeting.

Everything that the animals in our lives do is intended to
assist us in our soul's evolution. When you understand this
about your pet, it can be easier to accept that your beloved
pet has passed away. But more on that later!

It's enough to know now that animals (both alive and
not) desire to help us individually evolve, as well as help
mass consciousness grow.

I have written a much more comprehensive book about this called *Animal Lessons: Discovering Your Spiritual Connection with Animals* (animallessons.com). You can use my five-step technique in the book to discover exactly what lesson your pet (alive or crossed over) is teaching you and what you can do about it.

Why is there so much pet loss right now?

Animals have incarnated here with us to be of service to humankind.

As we're all experiencing, many animals are crossing over now. From unexpected accidents to longstanding illnesses, for many of us, it feels like the rate of pet death is picking up.

Animals have incarnated here with us to be of service to humankind. When I have connected with animals to ask about this, they're specific about sharing the phrase, "Of Service." This phrase does not mean subservient. Instead, being "of service" is an animal's divine honor. They are rescuing us by modeling and providing opportunities for us to rise to the occasion of love for all. My dog Kelso defined his purpose like this:

"Danielle, my job is to help people everywhere get as close as they can to mastering unconditional love."

Animals know that people avoid making changes until it becomes necessary. No one wakes up in the morning thinking, "Hey! Everything in my life is going great! I think I will do things differently today!" In fact, most people cling to their comfort zone, even if it's uncomfortable, because it's what they know.

There are two significant reasons behind the pet and animal deaths we're experiencing right now.

First, as I talked about earlier in this chapter, on an individual level, your pet may "act up" to draw your attention to the exact place you need to evolve. But this is also occurring globally, where animals are sacrificing themselves through widespread animal abuse, suffering, and other deathly experiences that draw the attention of hundreds of thousands of people all at once. (They aren't afraid of dying for the big-picture evolution of the human soul.) All this discomfort is an opportunity for change and growth in humans.

The second reason there is so much pet death right now is that when an animal completes the job they incarnated here to do, they move on to the next step in their soul's journey: their death. Many of the animals that have been with us for the past five, ten, and fifteen years have taken us as far as they can from within their physical body, and their passing indicates they're simply moving on to the next stage (the Other Side) where they can continue their relationship with us more effectively.

While you may be devastated at the loss of your beloved pet, perhaps knowing that their passing indicates something positive and wonderful that has occurred between the two of you can ease the pain in your heart a little bit.

Did I really choose my pet?

Do you feel like you actually chose your pet? Have you wondered if, somehow, your animal chose you? Many of us feel this way, and for good reason! The specific animals we connect with are pre-determined to be there.

Before you incarnated into this lifetime, your soul had a plan around which lessons you would be working on (your soul considers this "playing" rather than "working on") in your upcoming lifetime. This could be believing you're good enough, worthy, lovable, or safe. This means everyone that comes into your life will be contributing to that lesson in some way, including your beloved animals.

Here's how it works:

Before we're born into this life, your pet's soul and your human soul got together to form a type of agreement. In my *Animal Lessons* book, I refer to this as a

Soul Lesson with your pet. On social media, I often refer to this as an Animal Soul Contract (because that's easier to explain in a 14-second video). But they are the same thing.

Using myself as an example, my human soul knew I would play with the idea of believing in myself in this upcoming lifetime. So, it made agreements with many animal souls that they would incarnate and become part of my life to help me with this. You can imagine each animal soul saying to my soul, "OK, Danielle's soul. I hear you, and I'll join you at some point in this lifetime to help you learn that."

So, when you're born, you already have a network of animal support behind the scenes birthing into existence too.

Although it's been decided by your soul and the animal souls beforehand who will be helping you on your journey, what isn't decided is how each animal soul will help you. It's all about free will. The animals that are meant to assist you will meet you wherever you are in your soul's journey. Whether you're at the beginning, middle, or end of your Soul Lesson, the animal will intuit that and create the appropriate situations to assist you along the way.

This intentional agreement between souls applies to your soul and every animal you are affected by in your lifetime. So, of course, your beloved cat is helping your soul evolve and is meant to be with you, but so is your neighbor's annoying horse, the pig you read about on social media, and the mice in your basement!

Those feelings of "We were meant to be together" are true, and yes, in a way, your beloved pet DID choose you; however, you also chose each other a long, long time ago.

CHAPTER 2

BEFORE DYING

Why did my pet die now?

Your beloved pet left your life as part of the evolution of your relationship with them.

As you now know, as you and your pet go through life together, your pet will take every opportunity to help you evolve your soul through their interactions with you (learn more about this in my *Animal Lessons* book). They monitor your progress through their intuitive connection to you to know how you're doing and adjust their focus based on what they see at the Soul Level.

Are you starting to love yourself more? Are you feeling more confident? Are you speaking up? Are you beginning to feel safer or more loved?

And all of this is wonderful, right? You've got this incredible being looking out for you, assisting with your spiritual growth, and doing everything they can to help you be the best person you can be.

But as you begin learning the lesson your pet came here to assist you with, something else happens: Your pet inches closer to completing their job with you. When you understand the Soul Level lesson they're teaching you, they can move on to the next phase of their soul's existence.

Yes, you read that right: A pet who has completed their work with you will leave your life. This usually happens through death so that they can continue working with us from the Other Side, although there are a few other options as well:

- Running away

- Being forced to go somewhere else away from you

- Disappearing

I know this is heart-wrenching to read, and I wish I could offer you another explanation. But animals are incarnating here with us to assist us. When they have lovingly given their assistance to the best of their ability, from within their physical bodies, they move onward.

You're probably thinking, "Well, then. I'm not going to do my Soul Level work with my pet, which will ensure that they never have to move on." It's a logical thought, and many of my clients have tried this. Unfortunately, it doesn't work. You can't avoid your Soul Lesson because when you try, your pet knows it and simply ups the ante. If your cat is helping you learn to speak up by peeing outside the litter box and you try to avoid doing the work around that, your cat is going to start peeing in your bed and your car . . . and anywhere else that will get your attention.

When you can embrace the fact that your beloved pet left your life as part of the evolution of your relationship, their passing begins to take on a different meaning. Instead of blaming yourself for having done something wrong or not doing enough, your internal conversation can become one of gratitude.

Love your relationship with the animal in your life and work where they want you to work. This is what they want for you at the deepest level, and this is what will make them (and you) happiest.

Do animals plan their passing?

An animal's spirit and body work together throughout their life into their death.

There are no accidents. Even an accident isn't an accident. Animals have shared with me thousands of times that they knew they were going to die and that they planned for that particular death at that specific time. The way the animal dies is the way the animal planned to die at the Soul Level. (If you need more information on the Soul Level versus the Physical Level, please read Chapter 1.) This includes being eaten by another animal, sickness, being eaten by a human, and even being mistreated.

I have never intuitively heard an animal say, "I wasn't supposed to die." When I'm connected with them, they have shared an awe-inspiring awareness and understanding of their passing that most of us could only dream of having. They pass when the time is right according to the big picture (read: universal) plan of why they incarnated here with us in the first place.

They base this plan on very particular factors that most of us are unaware of. The three of the most important factors animals consider when planning their passing are:

- The Lesson

- The Method

- Who's Who

Let's look at each piece individually so you can understand what is behind a pet's death.

The LESSON

As you know by now, your pet came into your life to help you somehow become a better, happier, healthier person. When we have mastered the lesson that our pet is teaching us to the degree that that pet can help us with that lesson while in their physical body, the animal will leave our life.

Where you are in the Soul Lesson with your pet strongly influences the timing of your pet's crossing. Please see my *Animal Lessons* book for more information on these Soul Lessons with pets.

The METHOD

Our animals use our human experiences with them to help us evolve, and that can include the way your pet dies as well. Although they have infinite ways they could pass (dying from an illness, accident, abuse, etc.), they choose very deliberately because each death creates a specific experience for their loved ones. They often choose a method of dying that can help them continue to grow and evolve.

Some animals choose very quick and unexpected deaths, while others choose long and drawn-out. Still, others may opt for lack of clarity for their humans around their passing. Whatever method they choose, there is something for you to learn regarding the big picture.

For example, let's say your dog was helping you learn that it's OK to say no to protect your well-being. Your dog may then die in a way that pushes you to make choices around that. (Do you stay up every minute of every night tube-feeding her, or do you ask your partner for help so you can take a catnap? Do you listen to your gut about her care or to your pushy neighbor?)

Your pet chooses different methods based on what they know will help you evolve the most at the deepest levels.

Think about the passing of your beloved pet. Can you see anything that you can learn? Does it spark an idea or a thought within you? This is a great way to honor your animal—by striving to know what they're asking you to learn.

Who's WHO

In addition to planning when, why, and how, animals also plan who will be with them for the moment of their crossing. Rather than looking at the physical world, they also consider the big picture here. That means, even though they may love you dearly, they may also know that you'll learn the most from them or that you'll have a better experience if you aren't with them.

So often, we feel like we failed our beloved pets because we couldn't be with them during that moment when their spirit leaves their body. Our pets, however, arranged that to happen that way because, at all times, they have their eye on the big picture.

Are animals afraid to die?

At the Soul Level (aka the space of great wisdom within all beings), animals view death and dying very differently than we do. We tend to think of it as an ending or maybe even punishment or consequence for a life gone wrong.

Animals express their feelings about death in the opposite way: Death is the next step and is earned for a job well done here on Earth.

At the physical level, animals get jealous, they don't understand why their human goes to work, they have tummy aches, and they do not want to die at any cost.

At the Soul Level, though, things are different. Animals have access to all knowledge about their passing, the "why's" behind it, and most importantly: They have no negative, upset or hurting feelings about it.

They don't have the same baggage around it that we do because they view death as the next step in their journey. At this deep level, dying is a rite of passage. It means they have done this tough job they came here to do, and they're moving on to the next thing. I always use the example of graduating from eighth grade to ninth grade. The animal is moving from one experience to the next.

I have done thousands of "Getting Ready for Passing Over" readings with animals and their humans, and every single animal was aware of their passing.

One thing that can stand in the way of a pet's passing going exactly as planned: the animal's concern for their human(s) and how ready those humans were for the upcoming death. Our animals may choose to stay alive a bit longer to help prepare their humans mentally, emotionally, or physically for their passing. In a reading, they'll say things like, "My human is going to have a tough time with this, so I'm going to hang around another month to get them used to the idea that it's time for me to leave." Or they may say, "I'm going to make sure that I cross over really fast, so my human does not suffer extra guilt."

Animals are brilliant at coming up with different ways of helping their human go through the crossing-over process to get the most out of it—including furthering their Soul Lesson. They use their bravery around death to their advantage—and the benefit of the humans around them as well!

CHAPTER 3:

PREPARATION

How do I know if my pet is ready to cross over?

Animals give us signs all the time, and there is one universal sign that many of us overlook, hoping our beloved pet will continue to live with us forever.

I'm often asked, *Is it time? Is my animal ready to cross over? Is this the sign? Is this thing that's happening it?* But how do you know when it's really time?

I've heard people advise that you'll know it's time when your pet:

- Hasn't eaten a meal for three days

- Starts biting everyone

- Sleeps all day

- Avoids people or animals

- Has a sudden drop in their blood pressure

But don't use these as guidelines! There is no way these can be universally applied to all animals. Thankfully the formula for figuring out if your pet is getting ready to die is much less complicated.

Here's the method I've given my clients to determine if the time has arrived for your pet to cross over. Please follow each step and don't rush through.

1. Hold the animal you're wondering about in your mind for a moment. Just think about them lovingly.

2. You know this animal better than most others, so really think about who this animal is. What do they love? What makes them happy? Imagine your pet doing these things. How do they look when they do these things? What emotions do you imagine they are experiencing?

3. Now, consider what it would be like for this animal if they could not do the "ultimate" things you just thought of.

4. Now, look at your beloved pet. Are they able to do the things that make them the happiest (that you just

found in question 2)? If they can't do those things, what is life really like for that particular animal? Is there a secondary thing that they now do instead that continues to make them happy?

The signs that an animal has completed their mission here are different for every animal. When you know an animal well, and you see that they aren't able to have the life that makes them THEM, it's a good time to start preparing yourself mentally.

Some animals, while they can't do the thing that used to make their heart sing, find a replacement "thing." So be sure to notice if there is a replacement thing! For example, my dog Kelso loved playing with a big blue ball, but as he got older, he couldn't play with it the same way. It would tire him out, and his teeth would bleed. He found a replacement with a small soccer ball, and it made him just as happy.

Every animal has different standards and needs, but when they fall below their own standards, they're sending you a sign that they're getting ready.

IS IT TIME? Guidance from your pet
Here are some additional ideas that may assist you in determining what to do in this very challenging time.

1. Your pet has an intuitive connection to you
   Your pet is always tapped into you intuitively, whether you're trying to send a message to them

or not. They're aware of your thoughts, feelings, emotions, and ideas. They're also able to subtly send you their thoughts, feelings, and emotions, and you don't have to be a professional psychic to pick these messages up. Knowing how connected your pet is to you may help you trust your gut more in your decisions around their health and well-being. What types of ideas have been on your mind around this?

2. Your pet's soul knows what is best

   Our pets have specific jobs with each of us: They want to help us heal, evolve, and align with unconditional love (they have already done this themselves) in addition to loving us. When they have completed their job with us, they leave our lives somehow. (You can read about this and how to work with it in my *Animal Lessons* book.) At the Soul Level, pets embrace death as a graduation in which they move from one level with a certain job to another level with a certain job. And when they've completed their job, they then move on to planning out their passing. Is there any feeling within you that that is what is happening here?

3. There are no coincidences

   Animals plan their passing at the (unseen) Soul Level. For example, is euthanasia showing up in various ways in your world? Is something else showing up in various ways? Trust that your pet can intuitively use your environment to give you the signs about what they want, how they feel, and what they want you to do. There are no coincidences—often, what you'd see as a coincidence is really a message from your beloved pet about the best next steps.

Whatever you decide, know that your pet loves you, and I love you too. Your pet thanks you for taking the time to make sure you're making the best decision for their greatest and highest good.

How do pets feel about euthanasia?

A lot of us worry about euthanasia. We worry that perhaps we waited too long or didn't wait long enough. We worry that it wasn't the right thing to do. We worry that our pet is mad at us because we helped them cross over . . .

As you now know, animals plan their passing. They plan when they'll die, who will be with them, and even what they die of.

I always imagine an animal with a long list of ways to die, scrolling through the list and saying, "Yes! That one will be the way that meets my and my human's Soul Level needs the best!"

Euthanasia is one of the options on that list. And luckily for us, if an animal has chosen this method, they often leave subtle and not-so-subtle clues that help us make the decision. For example, perhaps it's been on your mind, but you weren't sure if it was right. Then you watch a TV show about euthanasia, and you overhear a conversation on the street where someone is mentioning it . . . these can be clues from your beloved animal, nudging you in their chosen direction.

Excitingly, when you think you've finally made the decision, you really haven't! You've just finally agreed to what, at the Soul Level, your pet has been working you toward!

How can I prepare for my pet's passing?

When our beloved pet goes through the death and dying process, most of us want nothing more than to ensure they're not suffering.

As an animal communicator, I've psychically connected with thousands of animals as they experience the death and dying process. Based on what they have shared with me, there are five things you can do to help your pet who is getting ready to leave their body.

Tip ONE: Treat your pet as normally as you can
Animals are naturally clued into how we behave, how we feel, our energy, and even our deepest thoughts. Many people react to this part of their pet's life by wanting to hide away with them, maybe by crying on the sofa a lot, or by watching

them like a hawk all night . . . but what do pets really want in this situation? Normalcy! Regular mealtimes and as many of the fun things they used to do with you as possible. It can feel jarring when you suddenly let go of all the routine and fun stuff. Even if you have to adapt some of those fun things (like carrying your pet to their favorite spot on the lake), continuing to do your normal, happy stuff as long as your pet can enjoy it assists them in feeling safe and comfortable.

Tip TWO: Manage your energy for your pet
Animals going through the death and dying process often want me to remind their humans to take care of themselves emotionally. When we, as loving, grieving human beings, don't take care of our energy (I'll show you how in a moment), we tend to dump our upset on our dying pet. Then, our dying pet has to manage their own experience and deal with our energy. What does that look like? It could be that you won't let your pet out of your sight or that you're holding them and crying and crying and crying. You could also be moving into extreme babying (animals don't enjoy being babied as baby humans do).

Here's how you can manage your energy better for your pet's well-being. First, before spending time with, or even checking on your pet, take a few deep breaths. Calm yourself. This doesn't mean that you can't cry if you need. But crying every single time you're together takes a lot of energy! Also, as your pet goes through this process, remember to eat well, drink water and generally take good care of yourself. Your responsibility throughout this process is to hold space for them, and it's tough to do that if you're feeling terrible or sick. I also offer many Energy Management techniques on my website: daniellemackinnon.com, including videos walking you through more techniques in my Be Open Community and on my YouTube channel.

Tip THREE: Allow your pet the space they're asking for
Some animals do not want to be coddled as they go through death and dying. Interestingly, many of us humans want to hover. When I am dying, I know I'll want my friends and family all around me, holding my hand and showering me with love (at least, this is what I think I want now).

Animals are different. They often ask for space as sometimes they want to be alone in this process. This isn't because your pet doesn't love you—it's simply about space. The act of letting go of the physical body takes some otherworldly concentration. This is why your pet may get spacey and seem out of it at some points. If you can avoid taking this personally with thoughts like, "They don't love me!" or "Why doesn't my cat want me around?" and instead settle into the fact that your pet just needs some space to go through this change, you'll be giving them the space they need. This doesn't mean don't check on or touch your pet; it just means leave space if your pet is asking for it.

Tip FOUR: Let your pet have the dying plan they want
Animals have shown me, through my intuitive communications with them, that they actually PLAN their passing.
(See the "Do Animals Plan Their Passing" question.) They
have come into our lives to do the job of helping us grow
and evolve, and when that job is complete, it's time for them
to move on. At the Soul Level, they don't view death and
dying as negative. Instead, they are moving from one level to
the next (like graduating from eighth grade and moving on
to high school) via a plan they've created at the Soul Level.

How do you know if you're following their plan? You do
what feels right. And what do you do if you don't like their
plan? There's no way around it—they are driving the bus
on their death from a very deep level. This means that you
can't make a mistake here. How it occurs, even if you think
you did it "wrong," won't be wrong. There's something more
to it. Your pet will feel comforted when you go with what
"feels" right to you—as that "feeling" is often their way of
letting you know what they want.

**Tip FIVE: Become aware of how this passing may be
helping YOU**
There is more to an animal than so many people realize.
They have deep, gracious souls that enter our human lives to
help us evolve our own souls. Yes, that's right! Animals use
our experience with them to give us opportunities to look
at ourselves with new eyes (you can read more about this

in my *Animal Lessons* book at animallessons.com). When they have done their job, meaning when they have helped you grow in the way they came here to help you grow, they typically leave their bodies to move on to the next place.

If your pet is getting ready to cross over, this symbolizes that the two of you have reached an important place in your relationship. Embrace this deep, Soul Level aspect of your connection with your pet and think about how the passing may be helping you at a more profound level.

BONUS TIP: Talk with your pet about your relationship once they pass

Did you know there is an "after your pet dies" relationship? There is a reason that I can communicate psychically with animals that have crossed over, and it's that they are STILL accessible. They hang out with us, watch over us, and even send us our next animal, all from the Other Side. They can also send you signs to let you know they're around, show up in your dreams, and even "talk" with you. Remember that your pet's death isn't an ending during this challenging time. It is about a change for both of you. Reminding your pet (which is simply reminding yourself) that you can still be in touch after this process ends can help solidify things for continuing your connection.

CHAPTER 4:

THE PROCESS OF DYING

What happens to the spirit as the animal dies?

Crossing over to the Other Side is a big job for animals. One of the last steps in this complicated process is the actual separation of the spirit from the physical body.

The separation process begins quite awhile before the actual moment of death. In my psychic communications, animals will often share an image of their physical body depicting part of their spirit still inside their body, while another part of the spirit is outside of their body, making its way outward to the Light (or heaven or the Rainbow Bridge or whatever you call it within your belief system). The spirit gets a nice head start in the dying process, potentially even months earlier than anyone suspects the animal might be dying.

The beginning of the process of disconnecting from the physical world occurs at this time when the spirit starts to move its way out of the animal's body. This disconnection is obviously required for an animal to completely cross over, but it can take months or even a year to complete.

Because the animal is less connected to the physical world, they experience less pain and suffering. (If you're distracted watching TV while someone is pinching you, you're less likely to be bothered by it than if you're in an empty room focusing on the pinching.)

This applies to all animals, including ones that:

- Are sick and dying

- Were accidentally killed/tragically killed

- Were eaten

After learning that this is how the process works, many of my clients have been able to look back at the time before their pet's passing and notice that their pet was more spacey or harder to control in the days or weeks before their passing.

For me, knowing that animals aren't all the way connected to the physical world when they are about to pass over made me feel better about the animals I encounter who are dying. This disconnection feels like a natural kindness in the world that I'm so grateful the animals have shared with me so that I can share it with you.

Here's what happens as the animal spirit finally leaves the body:

Step 1: Decisions, Decisions, Decisions
The animal chooses the time, location, method, and all other details about their upcoming passing. We've covered this extensively in earlier chapters.

Step 2: Begin the Separation of Spirit and Body
Regardless of how the animal will cross over, the animal's spirit begins leaving their body before the actual moment of death. This head start means the more disconnected the animal's spirit is from their body, the less they "feel" in their physical body as they pass. The spirit simply starts leaving the animal's body through their bottom.

Step 3: The Rally
It's a big job for an animal to cross to the Other Side, and it requires a lot of energy to complete. The last step in the process before the soul can finally leave the body comes through this energy surge. Sometimes (although not always), the animal spirit needs to rally a bigger energetic push to finally leave the body. That surge can come through an obvious source, like a fatal occurrence, but it can come through other places as well, such as:

- A physical experience like a seizure or getting hit by a car

- Euthanasia

- The seeming "fighting" that can sometimes occur during euthanasia

- The "I'm suddenly totally fine!" thing that happens with some animals right before they die

That final rally, or energy surge, in whatever form it comes, acts as the last push to separate the animal's physical body and spirit.

Step 4: The Soul Leaves the Body
With the help of the rally, the soul can finally fully detach from the animal's body. This means that all energetic connections to that body have been severed, and your pet is no longer "there." There is no more pain, no more discomfort and no more emotions to be found within the body. This also means that the animal has released any attachment to pain, bad experiences, and suffering.

I have connected with many animals around their passing, and they often show me an image of themselves, looking down on their empty body. This isn't a negative image, though. They always seem to intend the image to be helpful for their humans to understand that they have fully left their body.

Learning these steps has given me comfort when I think about an animal that has died. In my work, I see so much trauma and pain with animals and their humans. It helps to know that they aren't experiencing their passing the way I feared they were.

What is the Rainbow Bridge?

Perform a Google search for, "Pets dying" and you'll be bombarded with posts, pages, and websites referring to the Rainbow Bridge. The phrase Rainbow Bridge is taken from the 1959 poem entitled, *The Rainbow Bridge*, written by Edna Clyne-Rehky (according to National Geographic Magazine in February 2023).

When both of my dogs died within three months of one another, I was given a copy of *The Rainbow Bridge* poem, and it comforted my wounded heart. The poem though is just that: a poem. It does not depict the afterlife in the same way the animals have shared with me. Here are the differences between the poem and the reality of the animal afterlife:

What is the Rainbow Bridge?

The Rainbow Bridge Poem Summary

- The poem labels the Animal Afterlife as the "Rainbow Bridge." When an animal dies, they go to a specific place called, The Rainbow Bridge.

- All animals, whether they are happy, sad, sick, hurt, sick, or lost go this same place. There, they are no longer sad, sick, unhealthy, or lost. At the Rainbow Bridge, they are restored to their original health, happiness, and perfection.

- Animals at the Rainbow Bridge miss deeply their special humans who have not yet died.

- The poem closes with the happy reunion of animals at the Rainbow Bridge and their humans so they can then cross the Rainbow Bridge together.

What the Animals Say

Just like in the poem, when an animal crosses over, the place they "go" is perfect and animals on the Other Side are happy, healthy, and whole. However, there is one big difference between what animals tell me and what the poem depicts: the animals I've connected with have described their "heaven" according to what their ideal life would have been like here

49

on earth. While this is not accurate, it is because this is all our human brains can grasp.

Let's say there is a dog on the Other Side who, when alive, adored running outdoors, was an avid swimmer, and loved chasing bugs. When I psychically connect with that deceased dog, they're going to tell me something like, "Here, there are logs to run over, and there is a river, and there are lots of bugs to catch, and I can run and run." Descriptions like this, with the animal in perfect health, experiencing their perfect day, help our human brains paint a very limited picture of the truth of the afterlife, but it is only a picture. The Afterlife is much more incredible than we can grasp.

Last, and most importantly: animals on the Other Side do not experience a sense of loss regarding their humans. It hurts my heart that so many people have read this poem and subsequently believe that their pet in the afterlife is suffering by missing them. According to the animals I've connected with, they do not miss us, nor do they do not feel lonely or abandoned because we are not there with them. From the Other Side they can visit us, and as you'll see later in the book, they are actively looking to reconnect with us by sending us signs and messages.

Who greets my pet in heaven?

This ubiquitous question has a simple answer that needs a bit of explanation. Who greets your pet in heaven? You do. And so do all your other special people and animals. Being dead or alive does not affect who greets who, and here's why.

When an animal incarnates into their physical body to be here on Earth with us, only a fraction of their soul incarnates with them. Most of their soul remains behind in the afterlife.

To explain this, animals have used this analogy with me: What happens when you shine a light onto a disco ball? Each little section reflects a bit of the light outward. Your pet's incarnation is just ONE of those reflections of light outward into their physical body. Their soul, though, remains seated where it has always been but now has a divine connection to the portion of it that has incarnated on Earth.

Human souls incarnate in the same way, which means that, even though you are here, more of you is there. And this is what makes it possible for you to greet your beloved pet when they cross to the Other Side.

Everyone in your pet's Soul Family is there to greet them as they return "home" to the Other Side. Your Soul Family includes all the people and animals that were important to them at any time in their lives and continues through your various lifetimes. This means that you may not even consciously know all the beings there to greet you or your pet, but at the Soul Level, you do!

CHAPTER 5:

THE ANIMAL AFTERLIFE

Will my pet forgive me?

Many of us spend time beating ourselves up for all the things we now think we should have done back when our beloved pet was alive. We believe we should have spent more time with them, should have given them better attention, and should have handled their death differently. For most people, the list of "should have's" is a mile long.

Luckily, your pet doesn't judge you as you judge you.

When your pet reaches the Other Side, they gain even more access to *the big picture* and are bathed in the unconditional love of all the souls in the spirit world. This means they gain even more clarity around why you made the decisions you made, why you did or didn't do certain things, and what you're working on in your Soul Lessons (with your pet and without your pet). Your pet then views every experience you had with them as an opportunity for you to grow.

The Other Side truly is a judgment-free zone. I know what people want to read here is that their pet forgives them for their mistakes. However, that's not really the way it works.

Your pet has such complete access to the Divine once on the Other Side, that they don't experience your "mistakes" as something to forgive. Their great understanding of the game we're all playing called Life allows them to see that none of your choices were personal to them and were instead part of your Soul's bigger learning experience.

To your pet, every "mistake" you've ever made has been in the name of learning your Soul Lesson—the exact lesson your pet was in your life to help you learn.

When dealing with the loss of a pet, we often lose sight of this: Our animals simply don't want us to spend our time feeling bad about all the places we think we failed with them.

They want us to be happy, grow, evolve, and learn from their passing. Not spend our time picking apart each thing we did and didn't do for them when they were alive.

And when you can finally believe that they hold only unconditional love for you, no matter what mistakes you made while they were alive, you're finally ready to develop a new relationship with them from the Other Side.

Do animals reincarnate?

I was wondering if my dog would reincarnate and come back to me. I miss her so much!

—Question from Danielle's YouTube channel

Reincarnation occurs after death when an animal incarnates into a new body and a new lifetime here with us on Earth. When we are missing our pet that crossed over, many of us spend time hoping that through reincarnation, we may have the opportunity to see our beloved pet again and alleviate our grief and pain.

On the positive side, our beloved animals do reincarnate, but for many of us, it's not the way we would like.

Our animals are part of our Soul Families. Everyone who is important to you in any way, everyone who has had a significant impact on you (positive or negative) in this lifetime, is part of your Soul Family. And that includes your animals. The animals in your life now have very likely been animals in your life before.

As part of your Soul Family, your beloved pet will reincarnate into another animal body, and the two of you will have the opportunity to be together again, but not until you have also reincarnated into another body.

The animal reincarnation cycle, according to what the animals have shown me, moves at the same rate as the human reincarnation cycle. I know that most people hope that their pet will reincarnate back into the person's current lifetime, though, so I am aware that this isn't ideal to read; however, there is an exciting reason for this:

Once they cross over, most animals shift their focus from helping us with our Soul Lessons in the physical to helping us with our Soul Lessons in the spiritual realm. From the Other Side, they send us messages, guide us, and help us continue working on those lessons so we can grow and evolve. Reincarnation back into a new body in your same lifetime would prevent them from being able to do their higher-level work with you.

DO animal souls reincarnate as human or vice versa?
Animals have mastered unconditional love, while humans have not. For this reason, an animal reincarnating as a

human would mean that that animal is going backward in their soul's evolution, and there's no reason for an animal to do that! Additionally, humans can't reincarnate as animals, as we've not yet mastered unconditional love.

Do pets care about what happens to their body after they die?

Is it true that it's harmful to keep pet ashes in the home because of stagnant energy?

—Question from Danielle's YouTube channel

When animals cross over, their energetic connection to their physical body is completely released, but their intention, knowledge, and love for us are not. They are very aware of our grief and upset, but on the Other Side, they don't feel that for themselves. They do, however, want to honor our needs and assist us through the process of our grief.

A pet focuses more on their human's grieving and life process than on their pet's deceased body. Even though, for them, they know that for many of us, their ashes (or gravesite, etc.) are the only connection we still feel to them.

It is because they know it's important to us (if it is) that they care what we do with their body after they've died. If you can honor your needs around their body, they will be happy that you did whatever you did. For example:

- If you feel connected to your pet's ashes and spreading their ashes feels like the right thing to do, your pet wants you to spread their ashes.

- If building a shrine to your pet has meaning to you, then your pet wants you to build that shrine.

- If you don't feel connected to your pet's ashes or gravesite, neither do they.

To your crossed-over pet, it simply matters that we, the humans, do what feels good and honors our relationship with them. They know how helpful it is for us to be able to do something that continues our connection to them. Often, scattering the ashes or holding their funeral is the first step in developing the new relationship with them they so desire from the Other Side.

CHAPTER 6:

SIGNS FROM
THE OTHER SIDE

Am I getting signs from my pet in the afterlife?

Your pet on the Other Side deeply desires
a relationship with you.

It can be challenging to trust that a sign is really a sign from your pet on the Other Side. Our animals that have crossed over are always sending us messages and signs. They want nothing more than for us to believe they're there and reconnect with them. Here are six signs that you may have been overlooking.

#1 Say My Name, Say My Name
The first way you can get signs from your pet in the afterlife is through use of your animal's name. One of my dogs on the

Other Side is Bella. She will often let me know she's around by saying, "Hi," through her name. For example, we will be watching TV, and I hear about a "Bella" on TV. A little while later, I'm reading the packaging at the grocery store, and the brand is Bella. Next, I get something in the mail and see the word Bella on it. When your pet's name, or a special word between you and your pet, keeps showing up, this is a sign from them. In this example, it's Bella simply telling me, "Hey, I'm around; I love you." That's all she's doing. And so often, that's all they're doing. They use signs so we can clue into their love.

#2 Smelly Animals

The second common way that signs from pets in the afterlife is smell. When Bella was alive, she was a stinky chocolate lab because she loved swimming and dirt and water and didn't like baths. She had a distinct Bella smell. Sometimes now, when I'm sitting at my desk in my office, the Bella smell just wafts by. That's it; it just wafts by. It is a simple reminder from her that she's around me.

Your pet could send you lots of different smell signs. From dirty dog smell to poop smell to hoof smell to the smell of their favorite toy . . . there are no "proper" smell signs. They choose whatever it is that you will most associate with them to make you remember them and think of them. Again, they're just letting you know they're around. They're just letting you know, "Hey, I'm here."

#3 Woof Woof

Animals love sending us signs as sounds. This could look like you're watching TV and think you just heard your cat in spirit's claws on the sofa. Or you could swear you heard your horse's hoof on the barn floor . . .

Sounds are a message for animals to send to us, but they can also be hard to trust. A lot of people will convince themselves that they made the sound up! When you can trust that you didn't imagine the sound, you open the door for your pet to send you more sound signs.

#4 Surprise!

The fourth sign is a little more challenging to wrap your head around, but that's because it occurs all in your head. Let's say you're hanging out in your backyard. Maybe you're playing ping-pong or mowing the lawn. For no reason whatsoever, you suddenly, without provocation, find yourself thinking of the animal that you love that's crossed over. Many of us struggle to believe this type of sign because it seems like you're just idly thinking of your pet, but the animals have an incredible way of pushing themselves into your thoughts. Those pop-into-your-head moments count!

#5 Eye Candy

Have you ever thought you saw your pet from the corner of your eye? If so, don't ignore that! It's one of the most popular ways that animals let us know they're around. This can also look like a quick flash, even right in front of you, but then, it's gone. Often when it happens, it will seem completely normal until you remember that your pet has crossed over and no longer lives in the home. You end up having this "feeling" that you keep seeing them around you. When this happens, trusting it will continue to open the energy for seeing them more often!

Each of these visual signs is our living proof that our animals on the Other Side are hanging out with us. When they do this, they're simply saying hello and checking in.

#6 **Sweet Dreams**

Did you know that one of the easiest signs for our beloved pets on the Other Side to send and for us to receive is a visit while we sleep? The visitation (which is what a nighttime visit like this is called) is different from the signs we discussed above because of control. With the previous signs, your job was to recognize when it happened. With visitation, you can request that your pet visit you before you go to bed. Visitation is different from a dream because a dream is just your brain working through your grief and loss, whereas a visitation feels . . . completely real. I have a step-by-step article on my website for my Dream Connect method that you can use if you want to dial in on the visitation.

How can I get a sign from my pet in the afterlife?

Your pet is sending you signs and messages from the afterlife, whether you're noticing them or not. So, getting a message from your pet on the Other Side is less about opening your psychic abilities and more about trusting the process.

First, your pet's spirit will never send you a negative message or sign. Even if they are trying to get you to realize that your partner isn't good for you, they'll give you the sign in a positive way. For example, a podcast might show up on your phone that talks about how to find your voice with cheating partners (or whatever the problem is), and the host has the same name as your pet. Yes, this is not so far-fetched in the world of signs from our pets!

Second, your pet will send signs that you may be the only one to understand. Whether it's a smell, a thought, or a "coincidence," the signs that our pets frequently send only mean something to us. This is why it's important to choose who you share your experience with. I would never share my animal communication experiences with someone who pooh-poohs everything! And a pooh-pooh-er will not see the value in a sign that only you understand.

Last, the more you can trust, the more you open the energy to get signs from your pet. It can be hard, but instead of looking at things as a coincidence, be impressed by your pet arranging for that thing to happen! It takes a lot of work for our animals to send us messages and signs (luckily, it's work that they love doing), so when you do finally get a sign, thank your pet even if you're not totally sure!

Now you're ready for my super-simple technique to get a sign.

1. Call on your pet in spirit by thinking about happy memories with them. The positive emotion you feel about them will draw them right to you.

2. When you're fully in the happy emotion, say something simple like, "Bella, please send me a sign you're around me in the next three days. I promise that I will not doubt any of your signs for the next three days or discard them as a coincidence. Thank you so much!"

3. Now, go through the next three days with an open mind and write everything down that happens!

If you want a much more in-depth method, on my daniellemackinnon.com website, search for the Dream Connect method. I've written it out step-by-step for you—thousands of people have had success with it so far!

Why can't I get a sign?

When I receive a message from one of my deceased pets, I'm always excited (even though I do this for a living), and I know almost everyone wants this, too. It's such a good feeling to know that those pets are out there, watching over us.

But what is happening when you are looking everywhere for a sign but can't find even one? What happens when you try all the techniques, do the prayers, read the books, and watch YouTube videos and still . . . nothing?

You're trying too hard!

Trying too hard isn't a common theme in our culture, is it? Usually, we're told, "Push through! Keep going, and you'll get it!" How often have you ignored your tiredness, insecurity, or emotion because you must achieve success?

In fact, we're often taught that the most successful are those who sacrificed themselves to achieve greatness.

In the world of signs, energy, and intuition with animals, this attitude toward receiving a message from your pet on the Other Side will backfire.

When we "try really hard" to do something, we are trying to manipulate things for a specific outcome. We have expectations of what our goal is, and we do everything within our power to reach that same goal.

But working in this way reduces the number of potential "goals" to just one. This means that if you're "trying" hard to get a sign from your pet on the Other Side, you're probably falling victim to your own expectations. You're expecting to hear a word or to see him on your bed in the middle of the night, but your pet is sending you a completely different sign!

This is an easy problem to remedy, though—all you have to do is let go of your expectations. You don't know what method your pet will choose to say "hello" from the Other Side, so let them do it however they want!

When you release expectation, the signs and messages will blow your mind!

CHAPTER 7:

GRIEF AND GUILT

What can I do about my grief?

You can't stop grief, but you can learn
to embrace it.

Grief. It doesn't matter if our loss is human or animal; if the connection was there in life, the grief will be there in death. Grief is a normal, natural process we all go through when we lose anyone we care about. If you're grieving the loss of your pet, you're probably feeling an even bigger pang, as so many around us simply don't understand how we could grieve an animal so deeply.

Over the years, I've given the following three steps to tens of thousands of humans grieving the loss of their pets. Before you tackle the three steps, please remember that the intention of these steps is not to stop your grief. That's impossible and unnatural. Instead, the steps will help you work *with* your grief so you can begin to understand it and move through it.

STEP 1: Separating the Emotions

Start paying attention to all the feelings that you're having in this moment. Grieving is a very normal process. When we're grieving, we feel sad. We feel lonely. We miss the physical presence of our beloved animals. We want to share with them in the way we're used to, and we can't. They're simply physically no longer around. We feel that change deeply as loss.

Unfortunately, many of us lump guilt into our grief. We feel guilty about our animal's life or something we did or didn't do "right." For many of us, the guilt can overwhelm the grief.

When we get to know which of our emotions are guilt-based and which of our feelings are grief-based, our experience becomes more manageable. (Be sure to read "Will my pet forgive me?" in The Animal Afterlife chapter above if you're experiencing heavy guilt.) So, start noticing when you're feeling grief. Simply, grief is feelings of loss, missing their physical presence, and missing that emotional support and focus.

At the same time, you can start noticing when you're feeling that other emotion—guilt. Guilt is sifting through all the things you did wrong or should have done better. It's wishing the past had been different and beating yourself up for things you now have no control over.

When we sit in guilt, we beat ourselves up for something that we cannot change (since it already happened). If you find that you're also feeling very guilty, instead of reprimanding yourself for what already occurred, what if you looked at what you could learn from the experience? What if you could take the lesson and apply it to your now? When you can do that, it opens you up to experience your grief without the added pressure (and often block) of being weighed down by guilt.

When you can differentiate between your grief and your guilt, your grieving process becomes clearer and often less painful.

STEP 2: Be Transparent

If you're not feeling OK about your pet's passing, avoid pretending. When we hold back or censor our emotions, we add frustration and loneliness to our already challenging time.

Let's say you helped your dog cross over with euthanasia. Showing a fake smile to the world while secretly grieving inside will lead to deep suffering. And suffering like this can contribute to a separation between you and the rest of the world, which is precisely the opposite of what would be most helpful right now. If you don't have anyone in your life that you feel comfortable letting see your real emotions, take this experience as a sign to find those people. Your beloved pet on the Other Side sincerely wants you to feel connected to them and to the living humans and animals in your life as well.

So, seek out your support people! There are others in the world who grieve just like you.

STEP 3: Find the Lesson & Grow

Animals often use their lives and their deaths as experiences to help us grow. When you step back and look at the experience with your pet, is there something in the big picture realm that you can learn here? When you can understand what that lesson is, it can help to shift from suffering and grief to gratitude and grief.

In my *Animal Lessons* book, I take you through my process to decipher with your pet what lesson they were or are teaching you; but for now, start thinking of the "thing" in your experience with your pet that has made the biggest impact on you. Was it that your dog was aggressive? Was it that you felt like you could trust this cat more than humans? Was it their passing, and how it happened? When you can find the lesson in the experience, it also helps to create a strong connection to your pet on the Other Side for future signs and shifts the focus away from grief or guilt.

What does my pet in spirit wish I knew?

A lot of people find me because their dog or cat just died, and they are feeling stunned and grief-stricken. Through that work, I've found that pets have a few universal messages for their humans. Here are three things your deceased pet wants you to know when they first cross over:

Your Pet Knows How Much You Love Her

As loving human beings grappling with our pet's death, we often start to go through the list in our heads of "I wish I had's . . ." like, "I wish I'd taken him for more walks" or "I wish I'd given her better food." Far and away, the biggest wish is, "I wish I REALLY made sure she knew how much I loved her."

Animals operate on a different vibration, though. Whereas we often judge each other based on our actions, animals tap into our hearts, connecting with us at the Soul Level. That means they are aware of more than our actions. They know our feelings, our intentions, and our deepest thoughts. No animal has ever told me they didn't know their human loved them! In fact, the animals are usually saying things to me like, "Yes! I definitely know! She told me every single morning!"

The Grieving Process for the Death of a Pet is Misunderstood

When a human family member dies, there are plenty of options for support. From counselors to self-help groups to book after book, support is everywhere. When an animal family member dies, although the grieving process is the same, there is a stark lack of understanding. How often did you hear, "It was just a cat!" That lack of understanding makes grieving a pet even more challenging.

Your animal that passed away wants you to find like-minded people who understand your grief, not insult it. You can't control your feelings of loss, and why would you want to? Our animals want us to learn, grow, and evolve through their passing, but we can't do that if we're trying to hide our sorrow from those around us who don't understand.

Find a supportive community (like my Be Open Community) or even just one supportive person with whom you can let all of your grief show. It's very hard to come to terms with your pet's death if you feel like no one understands you!

When to Contact an Animal Communicator
Animals can start communicating psychically from the Other Side within a few days or hours, but it doesn't mean that right after your pet's death is the best time to hire an animal communicator. This is because of you, not your pet.

Imagine that you're in an animal communication reading, and all this helpful information is coming through from your pet, but you're crying too hard to receive it. Before hiring an AC, be sure that you'll be composed enough to hear what your pet is saying. Most people need at least a month to bring themselves to a place where they can get the most out of the reading with their pet.

The more conscious you are about your pet's passing, the more it will assist your grieving process. This will open the space for an incredible animal communication reading.

Do pets mourn?

'm often asked if animals grieve, so I've connected with hundreds of animals to ask. The more I delved into animals and the animal afterlife, the more fascinated I became with their grief.

Animals grieve. They just don't grieve like we grieve. For us, when an animal dies, we miss their physical presence the most, as well as the connected feeling, the emotional support, and the ability to create, grow and evolve the relationship with them.

Animals, because they are much more connected to the world of spirit than we are, miss the physical presence of their human or animal friend. So, when an animal is grieving, they are grieving the change to their physical life.

In this sense, they have less to grieve. They can still connect with, see, and even share with their friend who crossed over, but the physical aspects are gone. However, they often end up with more to grieve because their human is grieving, and the "normalcy" of their prior physical world and time together has flown out the window due to their human's emotions.

When we grieve, we are sad. We stay in bed. We don't do our usual things. We may spend a lot of time crying and discover that it's hard to find joy in regular things. But we forget that our pet that is still here really needs these things from us!

When a dog that is used to getting two walks a day with you and his dog friend gets only one walk a week now because their human is in such grief, it can be hard for the dog. After all, our animals feel our emotions and thoughts every minute of every day!

If you're finding that your pet seems to be in deep, deep grief, look at your own grief. Have you stepped out of your animal's life? Are you feeling badly for spending time with them because the other one has passed over? Is there anything keeping you from enjoying the pet who is still here?

For our animals, we ARE their environment. When their environment goes wonky, they react. They miss what they had.

If you're in this situation, take some time to develop your new routine with your pet that is still here. Perhaps it will be a completely different routine or perhaps it will look mostly the same. Just remember that it's important to have a routine with your pet who is still here!

What can I say to my friend whose pet died?

Everyone handles when a pet dies differently, so it's important to know each grieving friend will need a different type of support. Here are three different scenarios to help you determine what will work best.

Support option 1: If your friend wants to grieve alone, there isn't much you can do other than say, "I'm so sorry for your loss. Please reach out to me if I can be of any help." Leave it there. For some, being alone is part of their process.

Support option 2: If your friend is asking for support, you'll have more options, but first, you must determine what kind of support they want. Do they want to cry on your shoulder? Then just give them your shoulder. A shoulder is a powerful way to be there for someone, but it can also be the most challenging for us because so many of us want to fix our friend's pain by giving them advice. Remember: Your friend is looking for a shoulder, not advice.

Support option 3: If your friend asks you to help them by asking questions directly and looking to you for an answer, then you have the most leeway for active assistance, but beware. Most people are not doing this. Most people simply want to cry on your shoulder and are not looking for advice. A friend who is asking for advice would say something like this, "Do you think I should do X or Y?" or "Do you feel like it would be helpful for me to talk with so-and-so or do XYZ thing . . ." They are not saying, "I just miss him so much! I wish I could make it better. . . ." That is not asking for advice (go back to Support option 2).

Before moving into what is helpful, look at these phrases that my past clients have found very unhelpful when trying to help your friend feel better:

- You can always get another one

- It was just his time

- It's not like this is a person

- You only had them for a little while

- Animals don't live that long anyway

- Most people would be over this by now

Now that we've determined that your friend is actively asking for your advice and you're not using any of the ideas in the bullet points above, here are some things that can help, using all that you've learned here in this book:

Help your friend see crossing over as The Next Step, like animals do

Remember that animals view their passing as the "next" phase (like graduating from middle school) based on having completed their work here with us. Unlike people, animals simply aren't afraid of dying. No animal has ever said to me, "I'm afraid to go," or "I don't want to go."

Help your friend handle guilt

If your friend is mixing their guilt with their grief, find out if they are open to separating those two emotions out from each other. This can lighten their emotional load quite a bit.

Help your friend understand an animal's capacity to forgive

Animals are completely aligned with unconditional love. It doesn't matter what their human did; unconditional love is unconditional love.

In the end, there isn't a lot of talking you need to do to support your friend as they grieve. Just offering your support in whatever way your friend asks is perfect.

Or send them to my YouTube videos :)

Resources

Danielle MacKinnon Website
DanielleMacKinnon.com
daniellemackinnon.com

Beginner Animal Communication Course
Learn Danielle's technique—no experience needed!
daniellemackinnon.com/SLAC-101

Danielle MacKinnon on YouTube
Danielle's videos dedicated to grieving pet loss
youtube.com/daniellemackinnon

Be Open Community
Danielle's private community of animal lovers
daniellemackinnon.com/beopen

***Animal Lessons* Book**
Animal Lessons: Discovering Your Spiritual Connection with
Animals
animallessons.com

Soul Level Animal Communication Reading®
Get a reading from Danielle's certified practitioners
daniellemackinnon.com/animal-communicators

***Soul Contracts* Book**
Soul Contracts: Find Harmony and Unlock Your Brilliance
daniellemackinnon.com/soul-contracts-book

Printed in Great Britain
by Amazon

41081951R00059